# PEGASUS ENCYCLOPEDIA LIBRARY

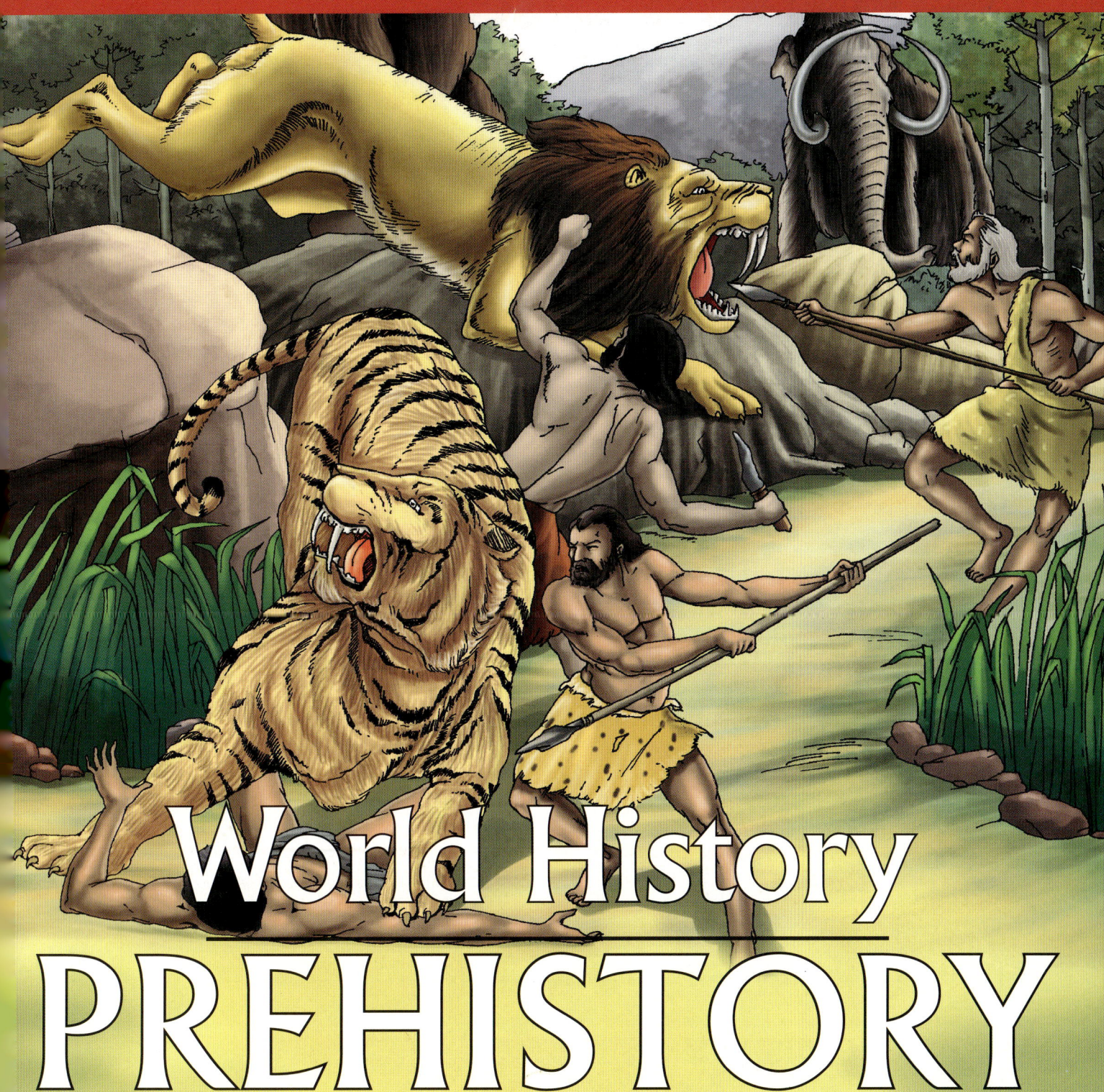

# World History
# PREHISTORY

Edited by: Tapasi De, Pallabi B. Tomar
Managing editor: Tapasi De
Designed by: Vijesh Chahal, Anil Kumar, Rohit Kumar
Illustrated by: Suman S. Roy, Tanoy Choudhury
Colouring done by: Vinay Kumar, Kiran Kumari & Pradeep Kumar

# CONTENTS

Evolution of man .................................................................... 3

Early Hominids ...................................................................... 4

Cro-Magnons ....................................................................... 13

The Ice Ages ......................................................................... 17

Darwin's 'Theory of Evolution' ............................................. 18

Prehistory and its ages ......................................................... 19

Bronze Age ........................................................................... 22

Iron Age ................................................................................ 23

Prehistoric art and music .................................................... 24

Prehistoric religion .............................................................. 26

Prehistoric medicine ............................................................ 27

Prehistoric animals .............................................................. 28

Test Your Memory ............................................................... 31

Index ..................................................................................... 32

# Evolution of man

In the simplest sense, evolution means the slow process of change from a simple to a more complex structure.

The evolution of man is a long and complex tale. Scientists and researchers are still trying to gauge the real story and they are successful to a large extent.

The timeframe for the stages of evolution of man from ape is not clearly known. A shortened chronology of what has been discovered from fossil remains is given for your knowledge.

**Prehistory is the time when written records were not kept and man was gradually evolving through many stages from ape-like beings to modern man.**

# Early Hominids

The word **hominidae** is used to describe the total member species of the human family that have lived since the last common ancestor of both man and the apes. A **hominid** is an individual species within that family.

The hominids were animal like humans that walked upright. It is believed that the earliest hominids lived around 4.4 million years ago in the forests of eastern and southern Africa.

## Hominid types

The species listed below are roughly in order of appearance in the fossil record. Each name consists of a genus name (e.g. Australopithecus, Homo) which is always capitalized, and a specific name (e.g. africanus, erectus) which is always in lower case. Within the text, genus names are often omitted for brevity. Each species has a type specimen which was used to define it.

### Ardipithecus ramidus

We begin with the category of early man called Ardipithecus ramidus which lived 4.4 million years ago. He was 4 ft tall and a bipedal (having two feet). It is thought that this species lived as forest dwellers.

# Early Hominids

## Australopithecus anamensis

Another new species called Australopithecus anamensis, was named in 1995 and was found in Kenya. This species lived between 4.2 and 3.9 million years ago. Its body showed advanced bipedal features, but the skull was closely similar to the ancient apes.

## Australopithecus afarensis

Australopithecus afarensis lived between 3.9 and 3.0 million years ago. He had an apelike face with a sloping forehead, a ridge over the eyes, a flat nose, and a chinless lower jaw. Australopithecus afarensis were 5ft tall. They were fully bipedal and the thickness of their bones showed that they were quite strong. Their built was similar to humans, but the head and face were proportionately much bigger.

## Australopithecus africanus

The Australopithecus africanus was similar to the afarensis, but lived between 3 and 2 million years ago. He was also bipedal and was slightly larger in size. His brain was not quite developed for speech.

## Australopithecus robustus

The Australopithecus robustus lived between 2 and 1.5 million years ago. His body was similar to that of the africanus, but had a larger skull and teeth. They also had a huge, flat face and had no forehead. The Australopithecus robustus never displayed any sign that they could speak.

## Australopithecus boisei

The Australopithecus boisei lived between 2.1 and 1.1 million years ago. He was smaller than the robustus, but with a larger face. He had huge molars (the largest measured 0.9 inches). Some authorities believe that the robustus and boisei were of the same species.

Australopithecus robustus

# PREHISTORY

## Homo habilis

Next is the **Homo habilis** which was also called 'the handy man' because tools were found with his fossil remains. **Homo habilis** was first discovered in 1959 in the Olduvai Gorge in Tanzania. They existed between 2.4 and 1.5 million years ago. The shape of the brain shows that they had the capacity of some speech. Males were a little over 5 ft tall and females were significantly shorter.

It is believed that Homo habilis were the first hominids to create and use tools. They probably lived alongside Australopithecus. Their larger bodies and brains must have given them a clear advantage.

Habilis had quite long arms, but was efficiently a bipedal. Very little is known of its life or mental capabilities, but its remains are often found with stone tools.

It is often believed that the activity of hunting was one of the chief causes of evolutionary change in early humans. Was Homo habilis a hunter and a successful competitor with the great predators of Africa that is with the lions, leopards, hyenas? Or was this species an opportunistic taker and a scavenger? Present evidence cannot answer the question, and it seems doubtful. Other Homo habilis remains have since been discovered at Olduvai Gorge. Male and female specimens and even one child have been recovered.

## Homo erectus

**Homo erectus** inhabited Africa, Asia and Europe some 1.6 million years ago and remained active in these areas until around 250,000 years ago. Homo erectus was the most long-lived species in the genus **Homo**. It seems that rather than simply going extinct, they appeared to have evolved into several species or subspecies in Africa, Asia and Europe. Their large brains allowed them to easily adapt to a wide variety of environments. Fossils of Homo erectus have been found in forests, plains and grasslands.

Historians often believe that Homo erectus began as gatherers but with the advent of time over many generations were converted into hunters. The women perhaps stayed close to home, where they cared for children, gathering nuts, fruit and leaves for eating.

It is believed that the men went for hunting in groups in search of meat. At first they only looked for animals that were already dead. With the passage of time, they developed tools such as clubs that allowed them to hunt and kill animals.

# PREHISTORY

## Wearing clothes

In order to keep warm, Homo erectus began wearing clothes. This began with individuals placing animal skins over their bodies. This came more advanced as they learned to stitch animal skins together using pieces of leather.

## Hominids leave Africa

Due to the paucity of evidence, there is a great deal of controversy among scientists about the exact time when prehistoric people left Africa and migrated to other parts of the world.

Some evidence suggests that Homo habilis may have been the first to leave Africa. However, if they did, it is unlikely that they remained there very long. There is however a strong evidence that Homo erectus migrated from Africa around 1.6 million years ago. Fossil evidence however shows that Homo erectus had arrived in Asia around 460,000 years ago and in Europe around 400,000 years ago.

## Birth of language

The first simple languages spoken by Homo erectus perhaps developed around 500,000 years ago. Before spoken languages were created, members of a group communicated with one another by grunting or through simple noises and sign language. The beginning of spoken language allowed the members

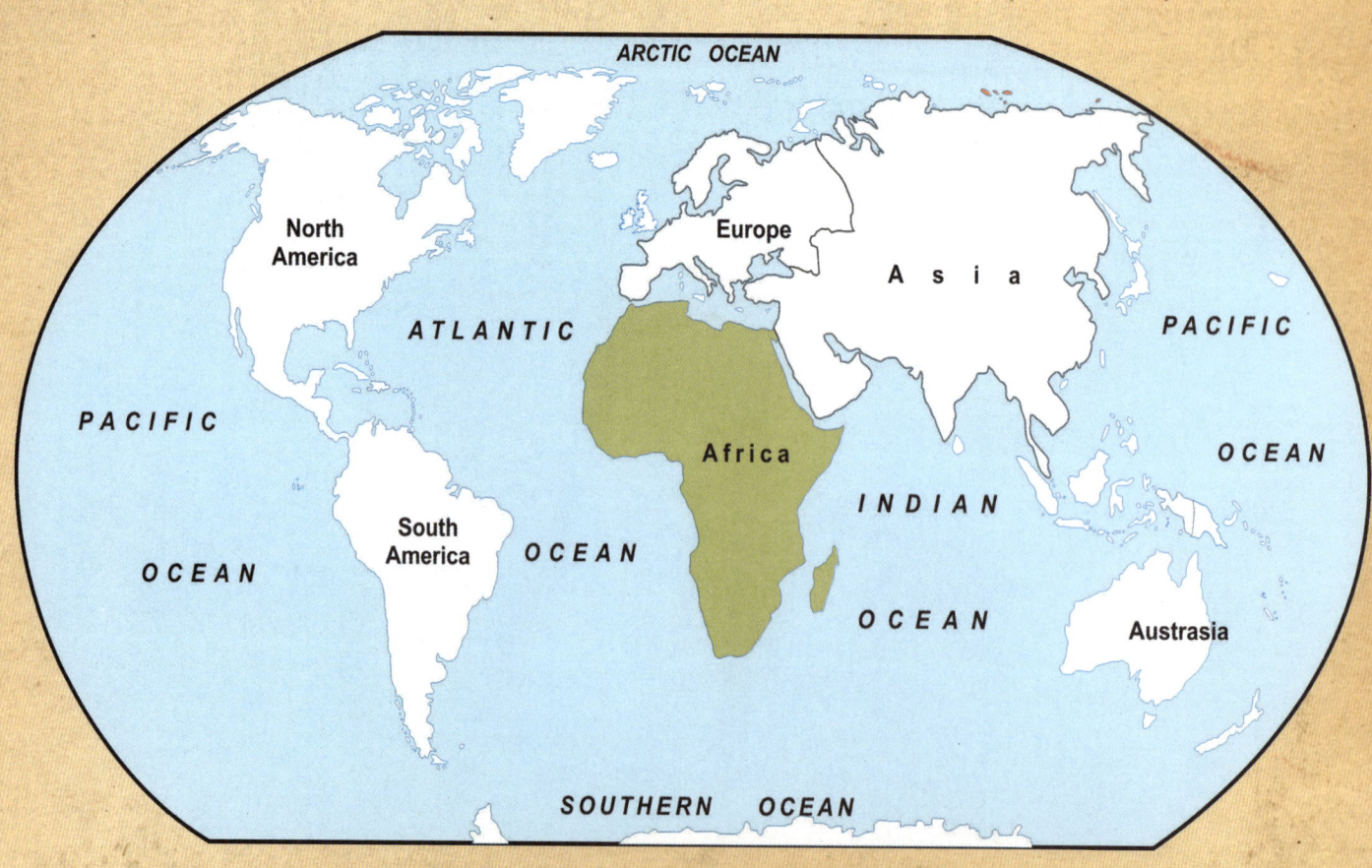

Early Hominids

of a particular group to exchange complex thoughts and ideas and pass on their culture from one generation to the next. Now groups could discuss plans, teach techniques of tracking animals or form religion and folklore. The knowledge of one generation could now be passed down to the next, expanding the human experience.

**In the ancient system of writing the characters were rough pictures of material objects or they are symbols of ideas. This way of representing ideas, which seems natural to man is known as ideographic writings and the signs are called ideograms.**

# PREHISTORY

## Change in physical size of Homo erectus

Among the early Homo erectus species, males were much larger than females as was typical of the early hominids. A million years ago, however, the size ratio of the male and female gradually changed and became roughly the same as in modern humans. Scientists believe that this size change in later Homo erectus signals important behavioural changes in the species. The increase in the size of females may indicate that they undertook the difficult task of giving birth to large-brained infants.

## Homo erectus—the tool maker

Homo erectus was an accomplished tool-maker and tool user. Hand-axes are widely distributed across hundreds of sites on three continents. The tools of Homo erectus are the first in the fossil record. Wooden tools and weapons are also assumed to be present in the tool kit of this species, but sadly none has been preserved in the fossil record.

He travelled out of Africa into the China and the Southeast Asia developing clothing for northern climates. It is noteworthy that only his head and face differed from modern man.

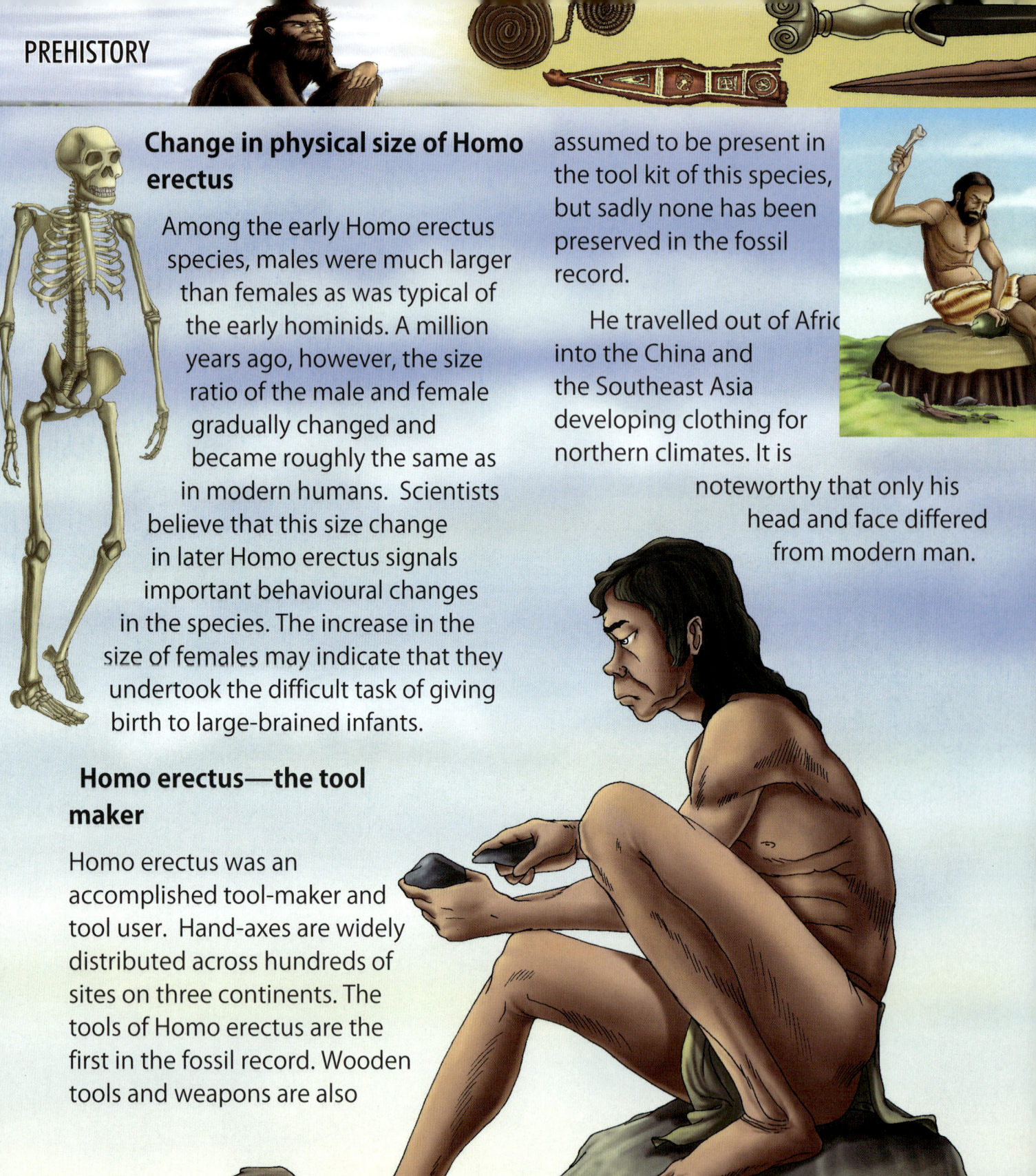

Early Hominids

## Homo erectus discovers fire

Homo erectus was probably the first species to discover and use fire. This very important milestone in human development occurred 1 million to 1.6 million years ago or perhaps even earlier. The discovery of fire surely helped humans to adapt to colder climates in Europe and Asia. The date of the earliest human discovery of fire will probably remain unclear.

## Cannibalism in Homo erectus

Some Homo erectus sites in China preserve evidence of cannibalism (eating other human beings) though many scientists believe that perhaps these acts were a part of some ritual rather than a carnivorous behaviour. One Homo erectus skull at Bodo in Africa shows signs of having been scalped!

The first scientific man to adopt the theory that all plants and animals including man are developed from certain original simple germs was Lamarck, a French naturalist in 1809. He acknowledged that God created matter, nothing more!

## Homo Sapiens

Homo sapiens (meaning 'one who thinks') lived in Europe and the Mideast between 150,000 and 35,000 years ago. The size of the brain of Homo sapiens was larger than modern man, but the head was shaped differently— longer and lower. His nose was large and extremely different from modern man in structure. He was a massive man, about 5ft 6 inches tall with a heavy skeleton. He was far stronger than modern man.

Homo sapiens is divided into two subspecies — **Homo Sapien Sapien and Homo Sapien Neanderthals**.

## Neanderthals

The first Homo sapiens are believed to have been the Neanderthals. Neanderthal people first appeared on the face of the Earth around 200,000 years ago in Africa. They were around 5 to 6 ft tall. They had thick sturdy bones, muscular shoulders, legs, arms and necks. The Neanderthals also had a large brain.

Like earlier hominids, Neanderthals made and used tools. However, the tools made by the Neanderthals were much more advanced than those used by their predecessors. They learned to create specialized tools for cutting and scrapping by chipping away the edge of a rock. They also learned to combine different types of stones into a single tool. They also discovered how to use a wide variety of soft and hard stones for specialized tasks.

The Neanderthal lived throughout a widely diverse climate and habitat. These people adapted quickly to new environments as they were used to migrating. Some lived in caves, while others built shelters out of branches and animal skins. Some even dug pits and covered them with branches, animal skins and leaves.

There is strong evidence that the Neanderthal had a belief in the after-life! Burial plots have been discovered where the dead were covered with flowers, buried with food and other necessary articles like tools which they would need in the next life!

## Homo Sapiens Sapiens

It is believed that modern humans like us first originated on the Earth around 50,000 years ago in Africa. These modern humans are referred to by historians as Homo sapiens sapiens. Within just a few thousand years these humans had spread to every continent across the entire planet.

When Homo sapiens sapiens migrated out of Africa, it is believed that they wiped out Neanderthals either by absorbing them through intermarriage or by destroying them completely through war and competition.

# Cro-Magnons

The earliest Homo sapiens sapiens were the **Cro-Magnons**. They are named after the location where they were discovered in France in the 1860s. Since their original discovery many other Cro-Magnon fossils and artifacts have been found throughout Europe, Asia and Africa.

The Cro-Magnons were taller than the Neanderthal, but they were not as muscular. A noteworthy fact about the Cro-Magnon is that they had much improved technologies, languages and cultures than those of the Neanderthals.

Cro-Magnons used other materials for making tools too. They used bones, antlers, teeth, and ivory. With these new materials, they were able to create sharper blades of their weapons, needles for sewing and fishhooks for fishing. Cro-Magnons also invented new kinds of weapons for long distances such as bow and arrows and spear throwers. Their invention of axes allowed them to chop down trees. Evidence has been found to show that early humans used some of these logs to make canoes also.

## Astonishing fact

One of the most important Cro-Magnon inventions was the needle. Needles were made out of animal bone. They were sharpened to a point at one end and had an eye at the other end.

# PREHISTORY

Homo erectus

## Cro-Magnon's social life

In the beginning, Cro-Magnon life was not at all different from the lives of earlier hominids. They lived in caves or temporary settlements and spent their lives hunting and gathering in small groups. As food sources increased, they started building permanent settlements. Many groups began building homes out of logs or stone. Smaller groups joined together forming larger groups. As these groups developed and the members increased, the need for law and order was felt; and so leaders were chosen to help enforce these laws.

Each group or tribe had their own methods for appointing their leaders. Sometimes leaders were selected through fighting. At other times, they were appointed according to religious beliefs or through inheritance.

A very convincing evidence for the existence of Homo erectus in Africa came with the discovery in 1960 of a partial braincase at Olduvai Gorge in Tanzania. This fossil, was excavated by Louis S.B. Leakey and is probably about 1.2 million years old.

Cro-Magnons

## Beginning of agriculture

For hundreds and thousands of years the hominids depended on nature for their living. Food came from wild plants and animals. A natural disaster could reduce the amount of food in the environment to nothing! Around 8,000 years ago a new way of providing food emerged. Early man learnt the art of farming. Instead of hunting and gathering food from the environments, humans learned to grow their own food for the first time!

Early civilizations first discovered agriculture when gatherers unknowingly dropped seeds from the plant that they had gathered. Soon they realized that planting these seeds in the ground could yield a crop!

# PREHISTORY

## Beginning of villages

With the beginning of farming and domestication of animals to feed a society, life became much easier for early humans. The population quickly increased from around 2 million humans on the Earth to more than 90 million!

People build villages along rivers or wherever the ground was fertile enough for crops to grow. Archeologists have found out that some villages that are believed to have been built more than 8,000 years ago. Ancient villages, such as Jericho, survive to this day.

## Inventions

As food was available in abundance, people had more time to devote to the development of new objects of their use. Better farming equipment, such as the ox driven plow was invented. The wheel aided humans greatly in transporting goods from one place to another. The loom allowed people to weave clothes. Tools for measuring the passage of time, such as calendars, star charts and sun dials were invented. This helped farmers track when the growing season would arrive, and when the right time to plant crops was. People learned new and improved farming techniques, like the use fertilizers.

Jericho

# The Ice Ages

During the last 2 million years the Earth has experienced four long periods of perpetual cold climate known as the ice ages. During each ice age, the average temperatures around the world had dropped dramatically. While the middle latitudes near the equator stay warm, the higher latitudes both in the North, and in the South get very cold, making life in these regions nearly impossible.

During these periods, massive glaciers formed which covered thousands of square miles. As ice sheets spread across the landscape they froze out plants and animals. As more and more water froze, the sea level decreased to as much as 300 ft. As sea the levels dropped, land bridges appeared between continents and islands.

Cooler temperatures forced changes on early hominids. They either had to adapt to their new environments, migrate or perish. Land bridges allowed hominids to migrate to new lands such as the Americas, Japan, Malaysia and Australia. Cooler temperatures hastened the development of clothes, and the discovery and mastery of fire.

# Darwin's 'Theory of Evolution

A 19th century English naturalist, Charles Robert Darwin was the first to present a scientific theory of how species have changed over time. On the basis of fossil evidences Darwin suggested that species were not stable and changeless as previously thought, but were capable of transformation into new forms. Most of the theories that supported the idea that species were immutable, were grounded after this.

Darwin's famous book, **On the Origins of Species by Means of Natural Selection** published in 1859, further advanced the theory that species came into existence by gradual changes over a long period of time. To explain the process, Darwin proposed two basic processes continually at work in nature. The first one he called **variation** which he said continually occurs within species and can be observed easily.

According to this theory, individual offspring of the same species, of the same parents, vary slightly from one another. In other words, the babies of particular parents are never completely identical. For example, members of the same litter of pups or the thousands of offspring of a pair of any marine creature are not identical to each other or to their parents. Darwin was not certain why this variation occurred. He only observed that it happened that way.

Darwin further noted that because of their different characteristics, the individual offspring were not equally successful in their struggle to survive and reproduce. He called this 'weeding out' process, the process of natural selection. **Natural selection** is the process by which species adapt to their environment.

The essence of Darwin's theory is very simple— new species have emerged on Earth from earlier life forms because of the two processes of variation and natural selection.

Darwin's theory gave us a good idea of how life came into being. It perhaps formed the basis of all the other later theories.

# Prehistory and its ages

Prehistory is the time when writing was not invented and so documentation of any historical event did not take place. Prehistory is often subdivided into three ages.

## Stone Age

The **Stone Age** refers to the period in which humans created most of their tools from stone. The dates vary according to the region of the Earth. In Europe, Asia, and Africa, many people think that this period might have existed around 2 million years ago.

The Stone Age is now subdivided into **Paleolithic**, **Mesolithic** and **Neolithic periods**, which in turn are often further subdivided. It ends at the time when metal tools began to be used widely.

## Paleolithic

The Paleolithic (Old Stone Age) period is the oldest part of the Stone Age in which the first use of stone tools occurred by the hominids (maybe 2,000,000 years ago). The Paleolithic is again subdivided into Lower Paleolithic, Upper Paleolithic and Epipaleolithic.

Throughout the Paleolithic, humans generally lived as nomadic hunter-gatherers. The Paleolithic was traditionally followed by the Mesolithic period.

The Paleolithic age ends with the development of agriculture, the domestication of certain animals and the smelting of copper ore to produce metal. As hunting and gathering gave way to agriculture, some people became artisans. Art (such as the cave paintings at Lascaux) and music also developed as people had more time for such creative pursuits. Human society emerged as more collective and inter-woven. People became aware that they faced the same challenges in survival, so co-operation was definitely better than competition. So a community identity became more important than individual identity.

# PREHISTORY

## Rituals and beliefs of Paleolithic age

A very common thought of Paleolithic man was that spirits inhabited not only animate but also inanimate objects. When they ate some animal parts, they believed that they acquired the qualities, say the cunningness or the strength of that animal. Fortune and misfortune was again explained by saying that the deities were pleased or angry. Objects were respected too. Some scholars believed that primitive magic was used to try to control the wind and the rain. Paleolithic people seemed to have prayed for the welfare of their community, rather than of individuals.

## Mesolithic

The Mesolithic or Middle Stone Age was a period between the Paleolithic and Neolithic periods of the Stone Age. The Mesolithic period began at the end of the Pleistocene epoch (usually dated as 1.8-1.6 million to 10,000 years before present), and ended with the introduction of agriculture. The Mesolithic period saw the birth of tools like fishing tackle, stone adzes and wooden objects like canoes and bows which have been found at some sites.

## Neolithic Age

The Neolithic period or New Stone Age was a period in human history when humans were still using stone tools, but they had started to settle in permanent settlements. The exact dates of the Neolithic Period vary, depending on which culture is under discussion. Several features of the Neolithic period are different from the Paleolithic period or Stone Age which directly preceded it. This period marked a dramatic

### Antler Harpoon
The antler harpoon was made to hunt large water animals. Between 20,000 to 10,000 years ago in Europe, the harpoon were used to hunt whales, seals and even swimming land mammals like reindeer.

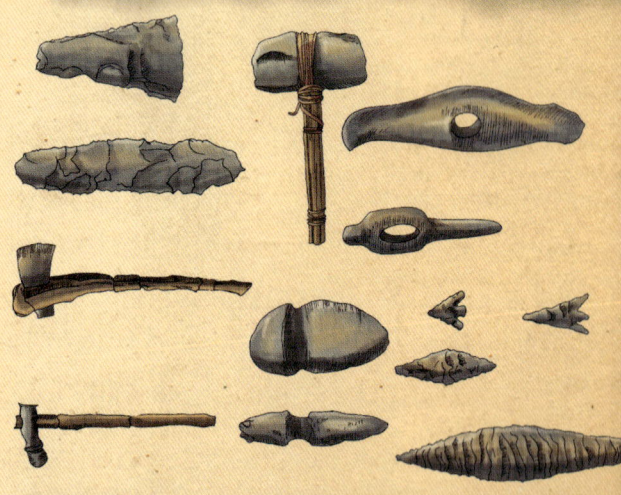

Neolithic men painting a cave

transition in the ways that humans lived and it is sometimes called the 'Neolithic Revolution'.

It is worth noting that the Neolithic period was marked by a transition from the hunting and gathering culture to settled farming. This transition allowed people to create permanent towns and villages and it paved the way to a more complex culture.

During the Neolithic Period, people began experimenting with crafts like pottery, weaving and other forms of utilitarian art. In addition to growing crops, these early humans also started domesticating animals to work for them and to serve as sources of food.

The creation of fixed settlements brought about some other major changes. The idea of private or personal property and land ownership began to be more widespread during the Neolithic period.

The concept of money began to emerge, and some societies unfortunately started keeping slaves as well.

The practice of religion and politics also became more complex during the Neolithic period as people had more time to invest in thinking about the mysteries of life. Early man also began to trade with each other and to develop complex uses for animal products like wool and milk.

Neolithic pottery

Neolithic men weaving

# Bronze Age

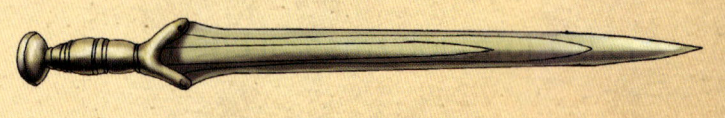

The Bronze Age refers to a period of time in prehistoric times where the usage of metals had advanced so much that prehistoric man learnt to make bronze—an alloy of tin and copper. It is the second period in the three-age system.

The Bronze Age primarily took place between 3500 BC and 1200 BC and is traditionally divided into the Early Bronze Age (c.3500-2000 BC), Middle Bronze Age (c.2000-1600 BC) and Late Bronze Age (c.1600-1200 BC), with an intensely advanced metallurgy which ultimately led to the discovery of ironworking.

The Bronze Age began 5,500 years ago in the present day areas of Turkey, Iran and Iraq which was also considered to be the cradle of human civilization.

The Bronze Age was important to mankind because it allowed us to create more durable tools and artifacts for our use. Bronze is preferred to stone for a wide variety of reasons; whether one is making a knife, an axe, armour, pottery or artwork, Bronze is harder and durable.

# Iron Age

The term Iron Age refers to the period in prehistory when iron working was the most advanced and sophisticated form of metalworking. The Iron Age is the most recent period in the three-age system in archeology for classifying human prehistory. It began in about the 12th century BC in the Near East, India and Greece, the 8th century BC in most of Europe and the 6th century BC in Northern Europe. The Iron Age ended in the 4th or 5th century BC in most of the world, but as late as AD 500 in Northern Europe. Iron always had an advantage over bronze. An iron sword could break a bronze sword with a strong blow.

The first systematic production of iron began in Anatolia (modern Turkey) and spread to both the East and West simultaneously. Anatolia was the centre of the Hittite Empire, which used iron weapons to conquer large parts of the Near East. In the Iron Age, much of the world was still occupied by hunter-gatherers and nomads, including the Americas, most of Africa and a major part of Australia.

# Prehistoric art and music

Prehistoric art can only be traced from the surviving artifacts. The rich art of the Paleolithic is replaced by a Mesolithic art which was very different from it. There were many changes in style as well as in meaning. The upper Paleolithic cave art depicts coloured drawings and expressive features of animals. A complete range of colours were used.

Mesolithic art in contrast was schematic; no realistic figures were present and only the colour red was used. This form was found in North Africa and the northern Mediterranean. The prehistoric art forms are mainly found in the form of petroglyphs and rock paintings.

## What is a Petroglyphs?

**Petroglyphs** appeared in the New Stone Age commonly known as Neolithic period. It is an abstract or symbolic image on stone, usually made by prehistoric people by means of carving or pecking. They were a dominant form of pre-writing symbols

> Petroglyphs (rock engravings) are images created by removing parts of a rock surface by incising, pecking, carving and abrading.

used in communication. Petroglyphs have been discovered in different parts of the world like Asia, North America, South America and Europe.

## Rock paintings

**Rock paintings** were painted on rock and were more naturalistic depictions than petroglyphs. In Paleolithic times, the representation of humans in cave paintings was rarely found. Mostly, animals were painted. The **Cave of Chauvet** in the Ardèche département, France, contains the most important preserved cave paintings of the Paleolithic era. The **Altamira cave paintings** in Spain show, among others, bison. **The hall of bulls** in Lascaux, Dordogne, France, is one of the best known cave paintings.

The meaning of the paintings remains unknown. The most important work of the Mesolithic era were the **Marching Warriors**, a rock painting at Cingle de la Mola, Castellón in Spain dated to about 7,000–4,000 B.C.E. The technique used was probably spitting or blowing the pigments onto the rock.

In the Neolithic age, evidence of early pottery and sculpture were found. The advent of metalworking in the Bronze Age brought another increase in mediums used for art, an increase in the variation of styles. It also saw the development of artisans, a class of people specializing in the production of art as well as in early writing systems.

## Prehistoric music

Prehistoric music is a term in the history of music for all music produced in preliterate cultures.

## Prehistoric musical instruments

It is possible that the earliest musical instrument was the human voice itself, which can make a vast array of sounds beginning from singing, humming and whistling to clicking, coughing and yawning.

It is most likely that the first instruments involving rhythm or percussion involved the clapping of hands, stones being hit together or other things that were capable of creating rhythm.

## Flutes

The oldest flute ever discovered maybe the so-called Divje Babe flute found in the Slovenian cave Divje Babe I in 1995. But this is disputed.

# Prehistoric religion

Prehistoric religion is a general term for the religious beliefs and practices of prehistoric people. More specifically it includes Paleolithic religion, Mesolithic religion, Neolithic religion and Bronze Age religion.

## Animal worship

A number of archeologists believe that Middle Paleolithic societies such as Neanderthal societies may have practiced the earliest form of **totemism** or animal worship. An important evidence in support of Middle Paleolithic animal worship is found in the Tsodilo Hills in the African Kalahari desert where a giant rock resembling a python accompanied by large amounts of coloured broken spear points and a secret chamber has been discovered inside a cave.

One eminent archaeologist puts forward a notion of a 'woman-centered' society with the prevalence of goddess worship throughout Pre History and ancient civilizations. However, this view is questioned by the majority of the scientific community.

Totem pole

Prehistoric men frequently performed a type of brain surgery that we today call trephination. Trephination was done by using stone instruments to bore or grind holes in the skull. Researchers do not know if the procedure was done to relieve demon spirits, treat skull fractures or remove bone splinters.

# Prehistoric medicine

Prehistoric medicine is a term used to describe the medicine before the invention of writing. The study of prehistoric medicine relies heavily on artifacts and human remains and on anthropology. It is clear that prehistoric societies believed in both natural and supernatural means of causing and treating disease. Early people blamed gods, evil spirits and sorcery for serious or disabling diseases for which they could find no rational cause.

Different diseases and ailments were common in prehistory. There is evidence that many people suffered from osteoarthritis, probably caused by the lifting of heavy objects which must have been a daily and necessary task in their societies. Injuries such as cuts, bruises and breakages of bone, would become very serious if infected. There is also evidence of rickets bone deformity and bone wastage (Osteomalacia) which was caused by a lack of Vitamin D.

In prehistoric times people lived for 25–40 years, with men living longer than women. Archaeological evidence shows that women mostly died at childbirth. Another possible explanation for the shorter life spans of prehistoric humans maybe malnutrition. Earths and clays may have provided prehistoric peoples with some of their first medicines.

## Surgery

Trepanning was a basic surgical operation carried out, predominantly in prehistoric societies across the world, although evidence shows a concentration of the practice in Peru.

## Medicine men

In the prehistoric times, medicine men (also witch-doctors, shamans) maintained the health of their tribe by gathering and distributing herbs, performing minor surgical procedures, providing medical advice and supernatural treatments such as charms, spells and amulets to ward off evil spirits.

# Prehistoric animals

There were a host of animal and birds species existing during the prehistoric times. Some of them were:

## Archaeopteryx

In 1861, paleontologists made a remarkable discovery in a German limestone quarry. Engraved in a 150 million year old slab of rock was a strange looking creature. It looked like a small dinosaur with a long tail, sharp teeth and clawed forelimbs. But it had feathers and wings like a bird!

It was named Archaeopteryx meaning 'ancient wing'. This prehistoric bird was hailed as a 'missing link' between dinosaurs and birds.

## Dire wolf

During the last Ice Age, dire wolves were quite common in the Rancho La Brea area. In fact, more dire wolf fossils have been found during excavations than those of any other mammal species. The large number suggests that these fierce animals, similar to modern wolves and dogs, hunted in packs. This wolf is very closely related to the modern timber wolf (also found at Rancho La Brea), but had slight physical differences, such as larger teeth and shorter limbs.

## Giant sloth

One of the strangest creatures of the Pleistocene Epoch was the Giant Sloth. They were huge relatives of today's tree sloth. Tree sloths are small, sleepy creatures that seem to move in slow motion. They are herbivores, eating very little other than leaves. They spend much of their life hanging upside down from a branch. The Giant Sloth in contrast, spent its life on the ground and used his size to reach up to eat in the trees. Leaves, their main food source, provide very little energy or nutrition and do not digest easily. Sloths may also eat insects and small lizards and carrion.

# Prehistoric animals

## Ichthyosaurs

It looked just like a fish. The strange thing is that they were not fish at all. They were reptiles like lizards, snakes, and crocodiles. Ichthyosaurs swam in the Mesozoic ocean when dinosaurs walked on land. To be precise, they appeared slightly earlier than dinosaurs. The earliest ichthyosaurs are known to be found from Canada, China, Japan, Spitsbergen and possibly in Thailand.

## The Woolly Mammoth

Woolly Mammoths are extinct herbivorous mammals. These mammoths lived in the tundras of Asia, Europe and North America. They are closely related to modern day Indian elephants.

Woolly Mammoths lived from (about 120,000 to 4,000 years ago), after the dinosaurs went extinct. Cave paintings of the woolly mammoth have been found in France and Spain.

They had long, dense, dark black hair and underfur, long, curved tusks, a fat hump, a long trunk and large ears. They were about 3.5 m long, 9.5 ft tall at the shoulder and weighed about 3 tons. The tusks were used for protection and for digging in the snow during the ice ages for grass and other food. This huge prehistoric huge animal probably went extinct because it couldn't adapt to the combined pressures of the climatic warming that occurred when the Ice Age ended, together with predation from human beings.

# PREHISTORY

## Mastodon

During the Pleistocene Epoch, from about 1.5 million to 10,000 years ago, the world grew tremendously cold. Huge sheets of ice covered the land. These harsh conditions seemed to encourage the development of giant mammals (probably because larger animals are better at competing for scare resources like food). Among them was the Mastodon. Mastodons were closely related to today's elephants. It was slightly shorter than an elephant, but more heavily built with upward curving tusks.

Both the mastodon and the mammoth were hunted by humans and this may have contributed to their disappearance after the end of the ice age.

## Sabertooth tigers

With their enormous, deadly-sharp canines, saber-toothed tigers are well-known to many people as frightening and ferocious predators of the Cenozoic era. Why they had such enormous teeth has been the topic of discussion among scientists. Definitely they used it in hunting, but opinions vary as to exactly how they were used. Some paleontologists have suggested that they were used to grab and hold onto prey. More likely, they must have delivered one crippling stab wound to its prey and then waited for it to die.

## Trilobita

Among all the well-known groups of extinct animals, trilobites probably rank second only to the dinosaurs in fame. Their fossils are instantly recognizable and often strikingly beautiful. In fact, prehistoric people liked them as much as we do. Although the last few trilobites went extinct about 245 million years ago, they are one of the best-known and the most-studied groups of fossil arthropods.

# Test Your MEMORY

1. Define evolution.

2. What is the Homo Habilis commonly called?

3. What is an 'ideogram'?

4. What do you mean by Homo Sapiens?

5. Which category of the primitive man invented the needle?

6. Name an ancient village that exits even today.

7. Who was Charles Darwin?

8. Name one of his books.

9. Name the subdivisions of the Stone Age.

10. What are Petroglyphics?

11. Name a prehistoric musical instrument.

12. Name 3 animals that existed in the prehistoric times.

# Index

## A
Altamira cave paintings  25
Antler Harpoon  20
Archaeopteryx  28
Ardipithecus ramidus  4
Australopithecus afarensis  5
Australopithecus africanus  5
Australopithecus anamensis  5
Australopithecus boisei  5
Australopithecus robustus  5

## B
Bronze Age  22, 25, 26

## C
Cannibalism  11
Cave of Chauvet  25
Charles  18
chronology  3
Cro-Magnons  13

## D
dire wolf  28

## G
giant sloth  28

## H
Homo erectus  14
hominidae  4
Homo erectus  7, 8, 10, 11

Homo habilis  6, 8
Homo Sapiens Sapiens  12

## I
Ichthyosaurs  29
ideograms  9
Iron Age  23

## M
Mastodon  30

## N
Natural selection  18
Neanderthals  12, 13

## P
Petroglyphs  24

## R
Robert Darwin  18

## S
Sabertooth tigers  30

## T
Tanzania  6, 14
The Woolly Mammoth  29
totemism  26
Trephination  26
Trilobita  30